RODGERS AND HAMMERSTEIN™

PIANO SOLO SELECTIONS

THE SOUND OF MUSIC®

Music by
Richard Rodgers

Lyrics by
Oscar Hammerstein II

2
Climb Ev'ry Mountain

5
Do-Re-Mi

8
Edelweiss

12
I Have Confidence

16
The Lonely Goatherd

20
Maria

25
My Favorite Things

30
Sixteen Going On Seventeen

34
So Long, Farewell

38
Something Good

44
The Sound of Music

41
Wedding Processional

ISBN 978-0-634-05043-5

WILLIAMSON MUSIC®
A RODGERS AND HAMMERSTEIN COMPANY
www.williamsonmusic.com

EXCLUSIVELY DISTRIBUTED BY
HAL•LEONARD® CORPORATION
7777 W. BLUEMOUND RD. P.O. BOX 13819 MILWAUKEE, WI 53213

Visit Hal Leonard Online at
www.halleonard.com

CLIMB EV'RY MOUNTAIN

Lyrics by OSCAR HAMMERSTEIN II
Music by RICHARD RODGERS

Copyright © 1959 by Richard Rodgers and Oscar Hammerstein II
Copyright Renewed
This arrangement Copyright © 1998 by WILLIAMSON MUSIC
WILLIAMSON MUSIC owner of publication and allied rights throughout the world
International Copyright Secured All Rights Reserved

4
4
1
1
1
3
1
5
8va
5
3
2
mf
cresc.
4

Broadly
3
rit.
f a tempo
cresc.
1
ff poco a poco rit.
3
mp
8vb

DO-RE-MI

Lyrics by OSCAR HAMMERSTEIN II
Music by RICHARD RODGERS

Copyright © 1959 by Richard Rodgers and Oscar Hammerstein II
Copyright Renewed
This arrangement Copyright © 1999 by WILLIAMSON MUSIC
WILLIAMSON MUSIC owner of publication and allied rights throughout the world
International Copyright Secured All Rights Reserved

f

mf
poco cresc.
Jazz Waltz (♩ = ♩)
molto rit.
f
Slowly (♫ = ♫)
p
rit.

EDELWEISS

Lyrics by OSCAR HAMMERSTEIN II
Music by RICHARD RODGERS

Copyright © 1959 by Richard Rodgers and Oscar Hammerstein II
Copyright Renewed
This arrangement Copyright © 1985 by WILLIAMSON MUSIC
WILLIAMSON MUSIC owner of publication and allied rights throughout the world
International Copyright Secured All Rights Reserved

animato
mf
rall.
expressivo
mp
animato
mf

meno mosso
rit.
a tempo
mp
L.H.
L.H.
simile
mf

f
sfz
Slower
8va
rit.
mp
mf
f
loco
8va
rit. dim.

I HAVE CONFIDENCE

Lyrics and Music by
RICHARD RODGERS

Copyright © 1964, 1965 by Richard Rodgers
Copyright Renewed
This arrangement Copyright © 2005 by WILLIAMSON MUSIC
WILLIAMSON MUSIC owner of publication and allied rights throughout the world
International Copyright Secured All Rights Reserved

3
mf
4
5
To Coda

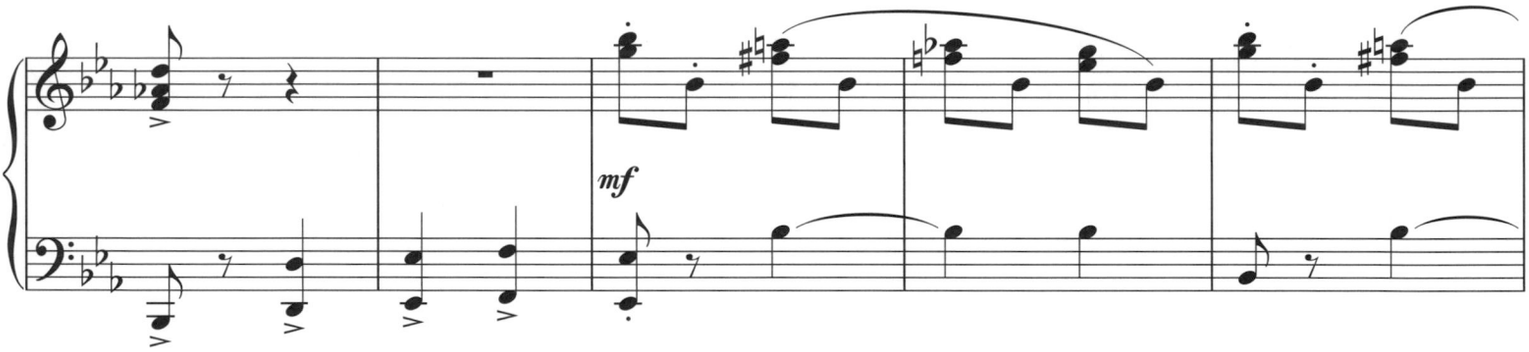
mf

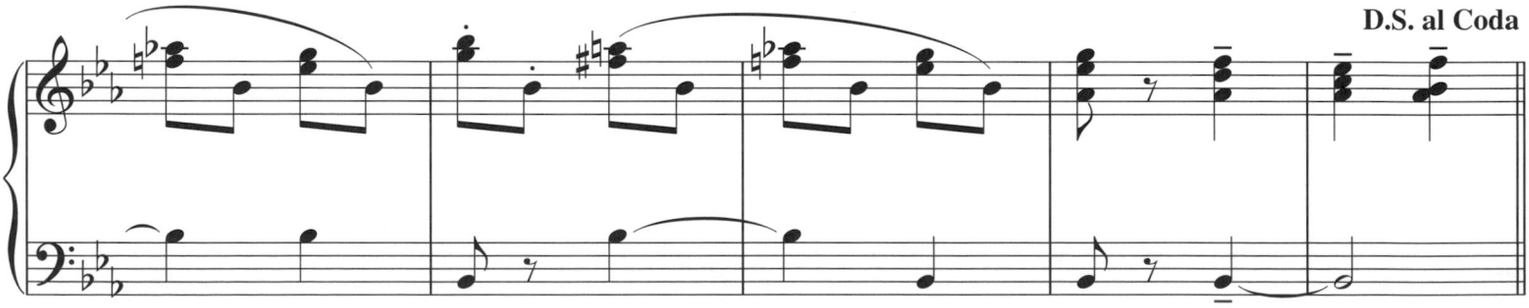
D.S. al Coda

CODA

mf
mf
f

THE LONELY GOATHERD

Lyrics by OSCAR HAMMERSTEIN II
Music by RICHARD RODGERS

Copyright © 1959 by Richard Rodgers and Oscar Hammerstein II
Copyright Renewed
This arrangement Copyright © 2005 by WILLIAMSON MUSIC
WILLIAMSON MUSIC owner of publication and allied rights throughout the world
International Copyright Secured All Rights Reserved

1
2
1
4
2
1
1.

2.
2
1

f
mp
cresc.
3
2
f

MARIA

Lyrics by OSCAR HAMMERSTEIN II
Music by RICHARD RODGERS

Copyright © 1959 by Richard Rodgers and Oscar Hammerstein II
Copyright Renewed
This arrangement Copyright © 2005 by WILLIAMSON MUSIC
WILLIAMSON MUSIC owner of publication and allied rights throughout the world
International Copyright Secured All Rights Reserved

2
1
5
3
1.
mf
2.

freely, rubato
rit.
Moderately, with a lilt

mf
f
Fine
Faster (♫ = ♫)
mp

1
2
1
D.S. al Fine
rit.

MY FAVORITE THINGS

Lyrics by OSCAR HAMMERSTEIN II
Music by RICHARD RODGERS

Copyright © 1959 by Richard Rodgers and Oscar Hammerstein II
Copyright Renewed
This arrangement Copyright © 1994 by WILLIAMSON MUSIC
WILLIAMSON MUSIC owner of publication and allied rights throughout the world
International Copyright Secured All Rights Reserved

mf

f

5
1
2
3
mf
mp
3
1
cresc.
3
1
4
2
1
f
1
mf
2
2
f
f

mp
cresc.
f

SIXTEEN GOING ON SEVENTEEN

Lyrics by OSCAR HAMMERSTEIN II
Music by RICHARD RODGERS

Copyright © 1959 by Richard Rodgers and Oscar Hammerstein II
Copyright Renewed
This arrangement Copyright © 2005 by WILLIAMSON MUSIC
WILLIAMSON MUSIC owner of publication and allied rights throughout the world
International Copyright Secured All Rights Reserved

1.
2.
mp
p
4
2
3

SO LONG, FAREWELL

Lyrics by OSCAR HAMMERSTEIN II
Music by RICHARD RODGERS

Copyright © 1959, 1960 by Richard Rodgers and Oscar Hammerstein II
Copyright Renewed
This arrangement Copyright © 2005 by WILLIAMSON MUSIC
WILLIAMSON MUSIC owner of publication and allied rights throughout the world
International Copyright Secured All Rights Reserved

rit.
A tempo (fast)
mp
fp
mf

1.
2.
p
fp
mf

Tranquil (slower)
mp
p
rit.
pp

SOMETHING GOOD

Lyrics and Music by
RICHARD RODGERS

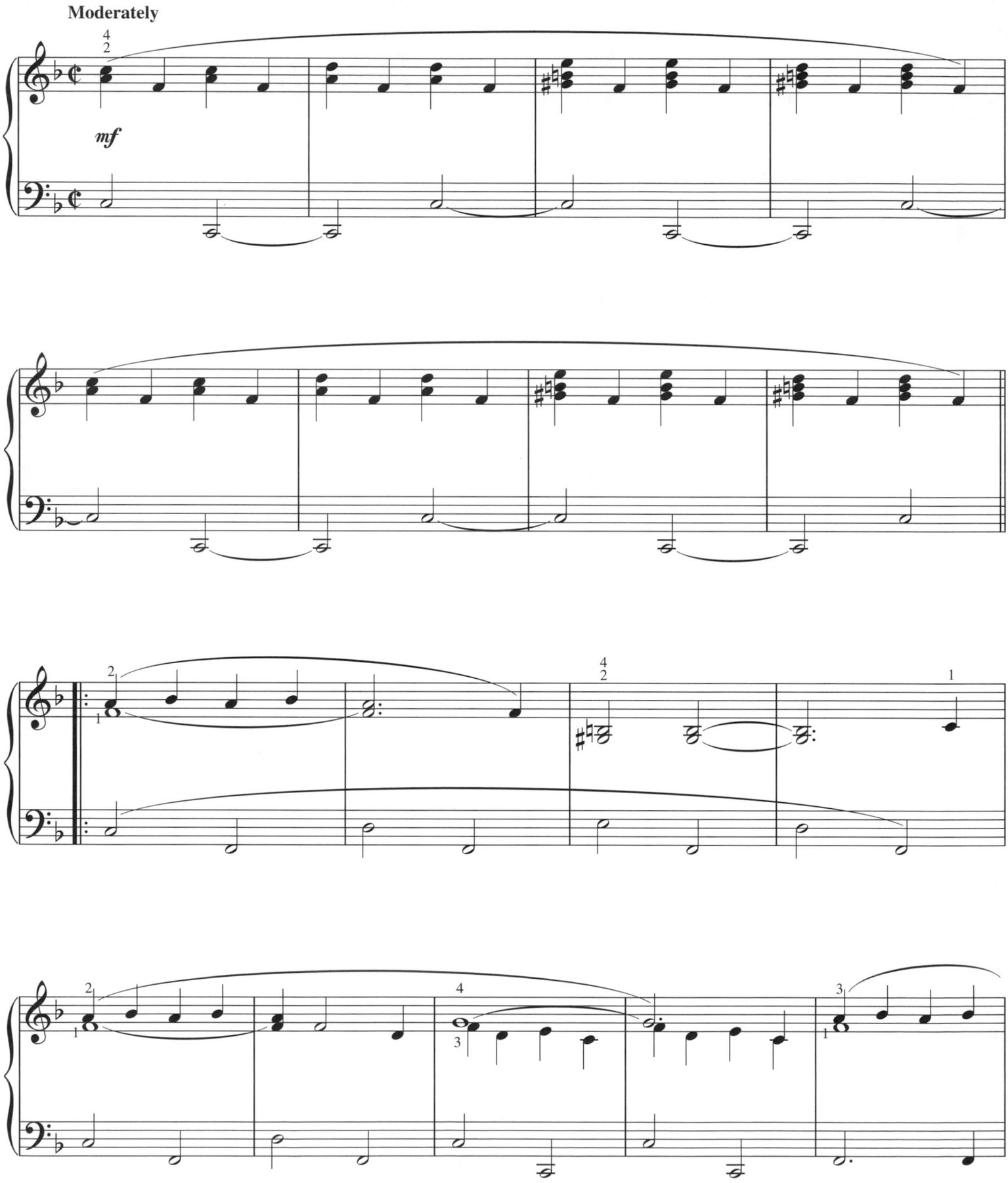

Copyright © 1964 by Richard Rodgers
Copyright Renewed
This arrangement Copyright © 2005 by WILLIAMSON MUSIC
WILLIAMSON MUSIC owner of publication and allied rights throughout the world
International Copyright Secured All Rights Reserved

1
1.
2.

WEDDING PROCESSIONAL

Lyrics by OSCAR HAMMERSTEIN II
Music by RICHARD RODGERS

Copyright © 1959 by Richard Rodgers and Oscar Hammerstein II
Copyright Renewed
This arrangement Copyright © 1998 by WILLIAMSON MUSIC
WILLIAMSON MUSIC owner of publication and allied rights throughout the world
International Copyright Secured All Rights Reserved

For the entrance of the Bride

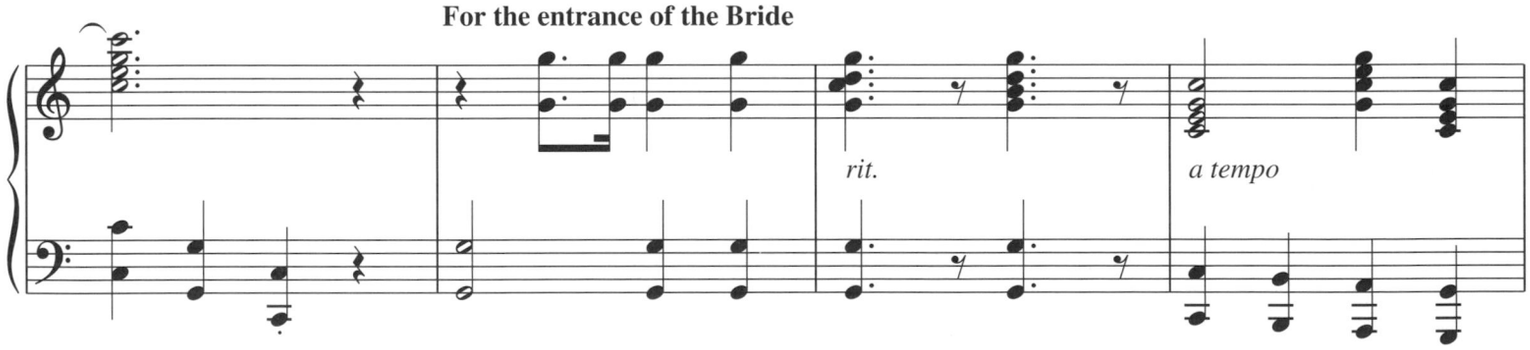

3
ff
rit.

THE SOUND OF MUSIC

Lyrics by OSCAR HAMMERSTEIN II
Music by RICHARD RODGERS

Copyright © 1959 by Richard Rodgers and Oscar Hammerstein II
Copyright Renewed
This arrangement Copyright © 1989 by WILLIAMSON MUSIC
WILLIAMSON MUSIC owner of publication and allied rights throughout the world
International Copyright Secured All Rights Reserved

f
rit.
a tempo

mf
a tempo
rit.
rit.